MIGHTY TRUCKS

Collector Card

MIGHTY TRUCKS

Collector Card

MIGHTY TRUCKS

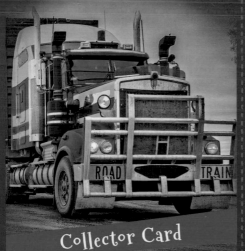

Collector Card

MIGHTY TRUCKS

Collector Card

LeTourneau L-2350

This vehicle holds the world record for the biggest earth mover.

SCORE

ENGINE POWER: 2300 hp	6
MAX. LOAD WEIGHT: 80 tons (72,500kg)	6
LENGTH: 66 ft. 7 in. (20.3m)	9
TOP SPEED: 12.3 mph (16.9km/h)	1

Liebherr T284

An awesome mining truck that carries really heavy loads.

SCORE

ENGINE POWER: 4023 hp	8
MAX. LOAD WEIGHT: 400 tons (363,000kg)	9
LENGTH: 47 ft. 7 in. (14.5m)	5
TOP SPEED: 34 mph (54km/h)	3

Renault VAB III

This vehicle can drive over, through, and up, and survive almost anything.

SCORE

ENGINE POWER: 320 hp	2
MAX. LOAD WEIGHT: 10 soldiers	2
LENGTH: 21 ft. 11 in. (6.7m)	3
TOP SPEED: 65 mph (105km/h)	8

Toyota Hilux

A version of this truck was the first vehicle to be driven to the North Pole.

SCORE

ENGINE POWER: 278 hp	1
MAX. LOAD WEIGHT: 1 ton (1390kg)	4
LENGTH: 17 ft. (5.26m)	1
TOP SPEED: 109 mph (175km/h)	10

It's all about...

MIGHTY
TRUCKS

KINGFISHER
NEW YORK

Life on the road

Some long-distance truck drivers spend most of their life on the road. At night, the driver parks the truck and sleeps in the cab.

FACT...

Many truck drivers drive for thousands of miles, sometimes over dangerous and remote roads. In winter, some roads cross frozen lakes.

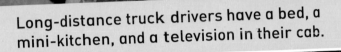

Long-distance truck drivers have a bed, a mini-kitchen, and a television in their cab.

This road in Bolivia is known as "Death Road." It is rarely more than ten feet (three meters) wide and has no guard rails.

Monster trucks

Special tracks with ramps are built for monster trucks to ride on.

FACT...

The original monster truck was created by Bob Chandler in 1974. It was called Bigfoot. One version of Bigfoot had 10-foot (3 meters) high wheels.

What do you get when you add huge wheels, great suspension, and bright colors to a pickup truck? A monster truck! A monster truck is a show truck designed for stunts and displays, such as riding over obstacles and crushing other vehicles.

Monster trucks crush trailers and sometimes even airplanes!

Rainbow colors

Most trucks are painted plain colors but there are some highly decorated trucks that would really put a smile on your face. Some are painted to advertise their contents in clever ways; others are painted just for fun.

Painted Pakistani trucks are known as jingle trucks.

FACT . . .

Truck painting is a popular form of art in Pakistan and Japan. Truck owners spend thousands of dollars painting their trucks and adding lights, statues, and mirrors.

Japanese painted *dekatora* trucks use neon lights and ultraviolet lights.

GLOSSARY

bulldozer A truck with a wide metal bucket that moves and carries rock and soil.

cab The place in a truck where the driver sits.

car transporter A truck that carries cars—usually between five and nine.

caterpillar treads A metal band of bumpy plates that move around sets of wheels to stop them slipping.

cement mixer A truck with a large mixer attachment that is used to carry cement.

concrete A mixture of stones and cement used to make roads and buildings.

container A large, strong metal box used to move goods by road, rail, ocean, or air.

dumper truck A truck with an open back that can tilt to pour out its contents.

excavator A truck with a digging attachment.

forklift truck A truck that picks up heavy loads with two prongs.

golf cart A small electric truck that carries players around a golf course.

loader A truck with a bucket on an arm that moves rubble or earth.

mine clearer A truck that clears bombs from an area.

parking gate The place where an airplane parks to drop off and collect passengers.

patrol buggy A small truck for searching an area in a war zone.

quarry An area where rock is collected from the ground.

remote Far from anywhere else.

suspension The springs and other metal parts that support a vehicle on its wheels.

tarmac A black, sticky mixture used to make roads.

troop carrier A truck that moves soldiers.

INDEX

MIGHTY TRUCKS

ROAD TRAIN

Collector Card

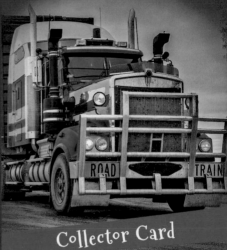

MIGHTY TRUCKS

ROAD TRAIN

Collector Card

MIGHTY TRUCKS

ROAD TRAIN

Collector Card

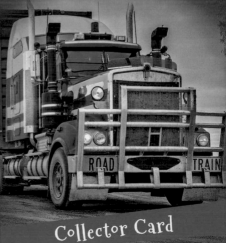

MIGHTY TRUCKS

ROAD TRAIN

Collector Card

Bigfoot 17

This monster truck can jump over 14 cars placed side by side.

SCORE

ENGINE POWER: 1749 hp	5
MAX. LOAD WEIGHT: 0	0
LENGTH: 18 ft. (5.5m)	2
TOP SPEED: 80 mph (128km/h)	9

Komatsu 960E-1

One of the largest mining trucks in the world.

SCORE

ENGINE POWER: 3500 hp	7
MAX. LOAD WEIGHT: 360 tons (327,000kg)	8
LENGTH: 51 ft. (15.6m)	6
TOP SPEED: 40 mph (64km/h)	4

Liebherr mobile crane LTM

The world's largest mobile crane has a 330-foot-(100 meter) long boom.

SCORE

ENGINE POWER: 670 hp	3
MAX. LOAD WEIGHT: 1.6 tons (1200kg)	3
LENGTH: 65.5 ft. (19.95m)	8
TOP SPEED: 50 mph (80km/h)	5

Belaz 75710

The strongest truck in the world uses two engines to move.

SCORE

ENGINE POWER: 6169 hp	10
MAX. LOAD WEIGHT: 496 tons (450,000kg)	10
LENGTH: 68 ft. (20.6m)	10
TOP SPEED: 40 mph (64km/h)	4